GUITAR
MADE EASY!

Acquisition and editorial: Nathaniel Gunod
Music typesetting: Gary Tomassetti
Cover, CD and interior design: Timothy Phelps
Recorded and engineered by Bar None Studio, Northford, CT
Cover photo: BP&V Photographic Associates
Fender Stratocaster courtesy of Fender Musical Instruments, INC.

Book: ISBN 1-929395-28-0
Book and CD: ISBN 1-929395-30-2
CD: ISBN 1-929395-29-9

Karen Hogg

TABLE OF CONTENTS

Karen Hogg lives in the New York City area where she performs regularly. She has been an instructor of guitar, banjo and mandolin at the American Institute of Guitar since 1995. An alumna of the National Guitar Workshop, she has been on the faculty there since 1991.

DEDICATION

This book is dedicated to my brother, Victor, who inspired me to pick up the guitar.

ACKNOWLEDGEMENTS

Big thanks and love to my parents, my brother, David Weintraub, Danielle Parillo, April Capone, Dan Canon, Nat Gunod, Amanda Monaco, Laura Gabbe, Denise Barbarita, Matt Smith, John Simpson and to all my students.

INTRODUCTION

Welcome to *Guitar Made Easy!* This book is an introduction to the instrument for the complete beginner. *Guitar Made Easy!* will give you the tools you need to start learning the guitar, whether it be on your own or with a private teacher.

A companion CD is available. Each example is demonstrated on the CD. If you have the CD, use it as a reference to ensure that you play each example correctly.

Practice every example slowly at first. Be patient and practice regularly and the examples will become easy for you to play.

Keep in mind that learning a musical instrument is a lifelong process. Becoming a great guitar player doesn't happen overnight, but with steady, consistent practice, you will see results. *Guitar Made Easy* will make a perfect companion for the beginning of your musical journey. Have fun!

Track 1

A compact disc is available for this book. Using this disc will help make learning more enjoyable and the information more meaningful. The CD will help you play the correct notes, rhythms and feel of each example. The track numbers below the symbols correspond directly to the example you want to hear. Track 1 will help you tune to this CD.

Let's get started! Below is a diagram illustrating the different parts of the guitar. Becoming familiar with each part of your instrument is an important first step towards playing it.

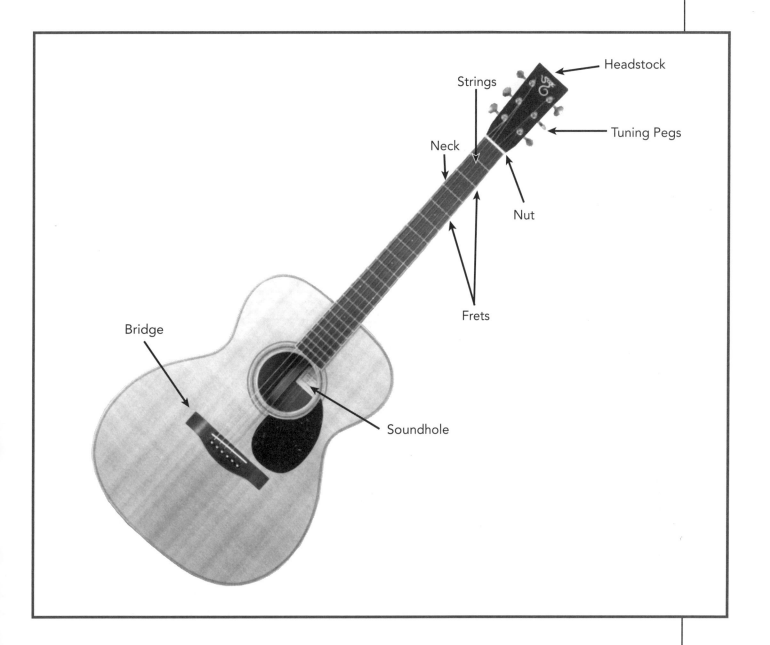

DIFFERENT KINDS OF GUITARS

There are three main categories that guitars fall into: the nylon-string acoustic, the steel-string acoustic and the electric guitar. Nylon-string guitars are used mostly for classical, flamenco and folk music. Acoustic steel-string guitars are used for many styles including folk, blues, country and rock music. An electric guitar is also used for a wide variety of musical styles including jazz, rock, funk and country. An electric guitar needs to be played through an amplifier in order to be heard.

Electric

Steel-String Acoustic

Nylon-String Acoustic
Classical

GUITAR MADE EASY!

BUYING A GUITAR

If you're getting started on guitar, your best bet is a steel-string acoustic or an electric guitar (nylon-string guitars have very wide necks which can be unwieldy for beginners). Just remember that if you get an electric guitar, you will also need to purchase an amplifier.

Quality beginning guitars usually cost between $200 and $300. You might ask, "Why do I want to spend that much money when I'm just getting started?"

In the end, you'll be glad you did. Guitars that cost less than that are often difficult to play and not properly *intonated* (they won't tune properly). It's better to spend a little more and get an instrument on which it is going to be easy to learn.

When it is time to go shopping for your instrument, it is a good idea to bring along a friend or family member who plays guitar. Please keep in mind that salespeople often get incentives to sell certain products, regardless of the gear's appropriateness for you.

SOME OTHER TOOLS YOU WILL NEED

1. A metronome
2. Picks
3. Strings
4. A music stand
5. A guitar strap

METRONOME

A metronome is a time-keeping device. Think of it as your own personal drummer in a tiny box. The metronome is a valuable tool in learning good rhythm.

PICKS

There are various gauges (thickness) of picks: light, medium, heavy, extra heavy. Experiment with different picks to see which feels best to you.

STRINGS

Strings come in various thicknesses. You can experiment and see what feels best to you. You will find that, although light-gauge strings are easier to play, heavier strings deliver a better tone. Keep in mind that if you switch string gauges, you will need to take your guitar to a repair person and have the neck adjusted. If it is not adjusted properly, the extra tension put on the neck by heavier strings can cause it to warp.

MUSIC STAND

It is important to have a music stand to help you maintain proper posture while reading music. This allows you to look straight ahead at the music while keeping your back straight. Otherwise, you may have to slouch over a table or another chair. Guitar playing shouldn't send you to the chiropractor!

GUITAR STRAP

A guitar strap is an important tool to have if you want to stand up while playing guitar. Make sure the strap you buy feels comfortable and doesn't dig into your shoulder.

Jimi Hendrix created a deeply soulful style of guitar playing that is as compelling today as it was when he first burst onto the music scene in 1967 with the release of his chart busting debut, "Are You Experienced?" The music world was astonished by the young rocker who would become the most celebrated guitarist of his era.

HOLDING THE GUITAR

It is important to have proper posture when playing. Bad habits in this area can lead to injuries down the line. Keep your back straight and angle the neck of the guitar so that your left hand has access to all of the frets.

HOLDING THE PICK

You should hold the pick between your thumb and your 1st finger. Try to keep a relaxed but firm grip on the pick.

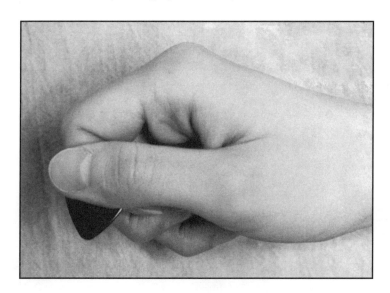

Now is a great time for you to turn to page 47, where you will find a quick overview of left-hand technique.

GETTING IN TUNE

Sooner or later, you're going to have to tune that guitar you bought. Various influences, such as weather changes or getting knocked around in the case, will cause your guitar to go out of tune. There are a few different ways to go about tuning:

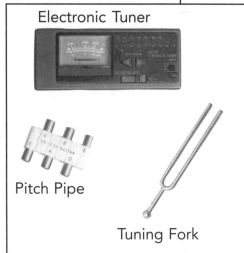

Electronic Tuner

Pitch Pipe

Tuning Fork

1. You can buy an electronic tuner. These are convenient devices that are especially helpful when you are first learning to get your guitar in tune.

2. You can tune to a pitch pipe or tuning fork. To do this, you play the pitch on the pipe or fork (usually an A), and then try to make the corresponding pitch on your guitar match that sound.

3. Many metronomes will produce tones (usually an A) you can tune your guitar to.

4. You can use Track 1 on the CD that is available for this book for a reference.

These are helpful tools, but they aren't always foolproof. Your electronic tuner could break or run out of batteries at an inconvenient time. You will need to learn how to get your guitar in *relative tune*. In other words, you will need to learn how to get all the strings in tune with each other, even when an electronic tuner or pitch pipe is not available. This takes practice, but over time your ear will develop to the point where you can easily tune your guitar.

PHOTO • AL PEREIRA/COURTESY OF STAR FILE, INC.

Eric Clapton was born in Surrey, England on March 30th, 1945. He has had tremendous success in the blues and rock world. His career spans work with such bands as Derek and the Dominos (Layla) and Cream (White Room). He has also had solo hits such as Wonderful Tonight *and* Tears in Heaven.

RELATIVE TUNING—SIX EASY STEPS

Here are the steps you need to follow to get your guitar in relative tune:

Step 1) First, you need to find a reference pitch—either from a tuning fork, a piano or another guitar. Use this to tune your 6th (lowest) string, E.

Step 2) Press the 6th string at the 5th fret with your left hand. Tune the open* 5th string to this pitch.

Step 3) Press the 5th string at the 5th fret. Tune the open 4th string to this pitch.

Step 4) Press the 4th string at the 5th fret. Tune the open 3rd string to this pitch.

Step 5) Press the 3rd string at the 4th fret. Tune the open 2nd string to this pitch.

Step 6) Press the 2nd string at the 5th fret. Tune the open 1st string to this pitch.

Don't be discouraged if it you're not immediately a tuning whiz. Your ear will take time to develop. If you keep at it, you will find that you will get better and better at tuning your guitar.

track 1

If you have the CD that is available for this book, you can tune your guitar to Track 1.

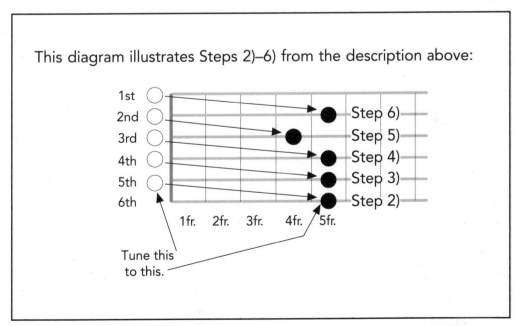

* An open string is one that is played without any fretted note.

THE GUITAR NECK AND THE MUSICAL ALPHABET

Learning the notes on the guitar neck is important. To do this, first you must learn the seven letters of the musical alphabet: A, B, C, D, E, F and G. These are the letter names given to musical notes. The alphabet repeats itself. The note after G is A. Knowing where all the notes of the musical alphabet lie on the *fretboard* (the top of the neck where the frets are) creates an essential building block to future musical knowledge. This book will introduce the notes within the first few frets of the guitar.

Let's begin by learning the names of the strings and becoming familiar with two different ways to illustrate the neck.

1st string = E (Highest in pitch)
2nd string = B
3rd string = G
4th string = D
5th string = A
6th string = E (Lowest in pitch)

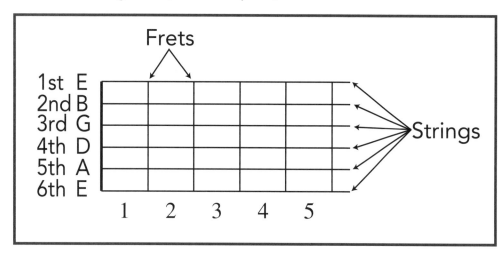

Memorize this!

As we ascend (move from left to right) on the fretboard, we move forward through the musical alphabet and the pitches ascend. For example, the open 1st string is E. The 1st fret on the 1st string is F and the 3rd fret is G.

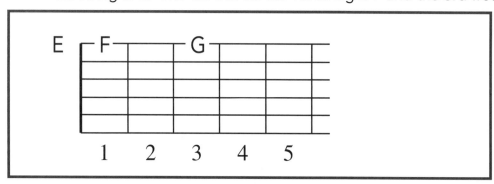

CHAPTER *Two* Introduction to Reading Music

It is a good idea to learn the basics of music notation and theory because this is how musicians communicate. This is the language we speak.

THE STAFF AND CLEF

Music is written on a set of five lines and four spaces called a *staff*. The staff is read from left to right.

At the beginning of the staff, there is a *clef*. Guitar music is written in *G clef* (also called *treble* clef). It is called the G clef because it encircles the G line on the staff. The staff is separated into *measures* by *bar lines*. A *double bar line* notates the end of an example or section.

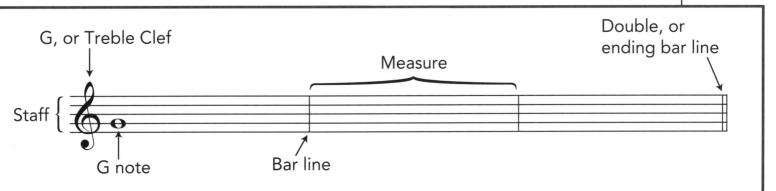

We read music by how the notes are placed on the staff. Each line or space is given a letter name from the musical alphabet: A-B-C-D-E-F-G.

RHYTHMIC VALUES

We can tell what the duration of a note is by its appearance. In music, durations are measured in *beats*. A *beat* is the basic unit of measurement of musical time.

Whole note = Four beats (four taps of your foot)
Half note   = Two beats

Quarter note = One beat

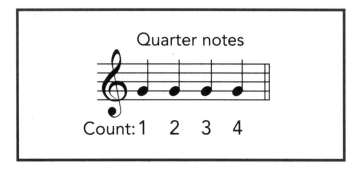

TIME SIGNATURES

A time signature is a set of numbers at the beginning of a piece of music that tells us how many beats are in each measure or bar. Most popular songs are in $\frac{4}{4}$ time. That means that there are four beats in each measure (this is what the top number tells us) and the quarter note gets one beat (this is what the bottom number tells us).

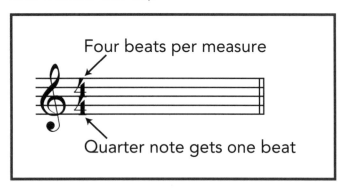

TABLATURE (TAB)

Tablature is a way of notating where to place your fingers on the fretboard of your guitar.

Tablature has six horizontal lines which are read from left to right. Each line represents a guitar string. The bottom line is the 6th string (low E). The top line is the 1st string (high E).

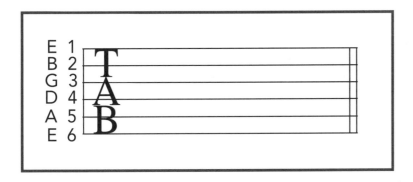

The numbers on each line represent which fret to play. For instance, the example below tells us to play the 1st string, 1st fret.

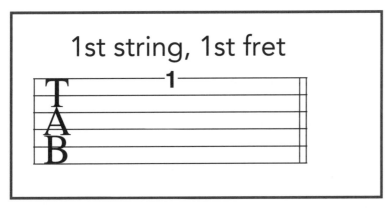

In many music books and magazines, tablature appears under the standard music notation. This provides a complete picture of the music. That is the system used in this book.

READING ON THE 1ST STRING

Here are three notes on the 1st string:

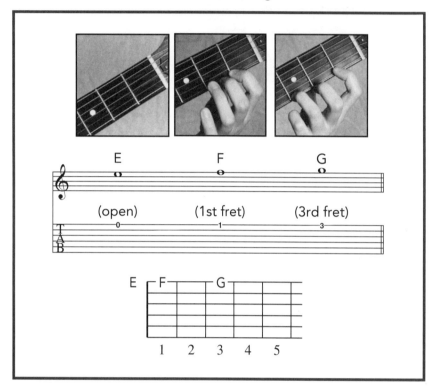

Example 1 is all whole notes. Each note is held for four beats. Count aloud as you play. Count as evenly as possible—use a metronome if you have one. Press your left-hand fingers just to the left of the indicated fret. Press as lightly as you can and still make a clear, ringing sound.

EXAMPLE 1

track 2

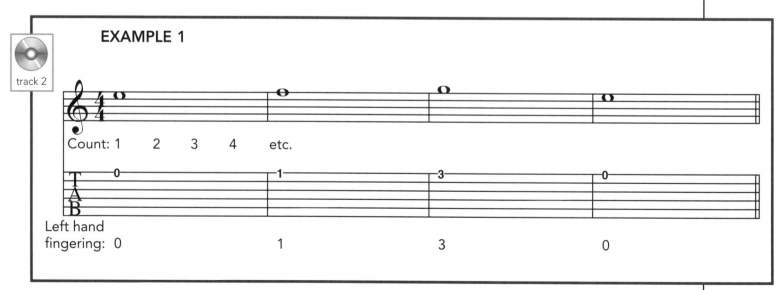

Example 2 consists of half notes and one whole note at the end. Remember that each half note gets two beats and the whole note gets four. Continue to count aloud.

EXAMPLE 2

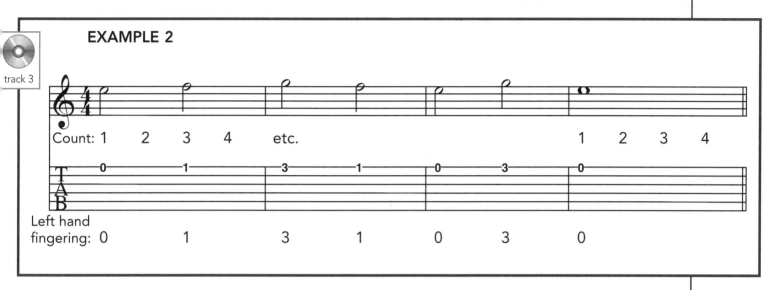

track 3

Count: 1   2   3   4   etc.   1   2   3   4

Left hand
fingering: 0   1   3   1   0   3   0

Example 3 will give you more practice with whole notes and half notes on the 1st string.

EXAMPLE 3

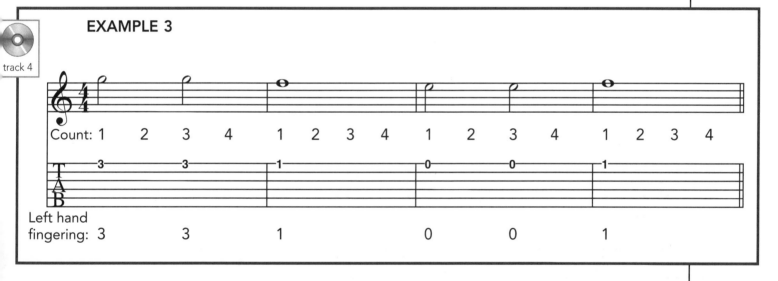

track 4

Count: 1   2   3   4   1   2   3   4   1   2   3   4   1   2   3   4

Left hand
fingering: 3   3   1   0   0   1

This example uses quarter notes. Each quarter note gets one beat.

EXAMPLE 4

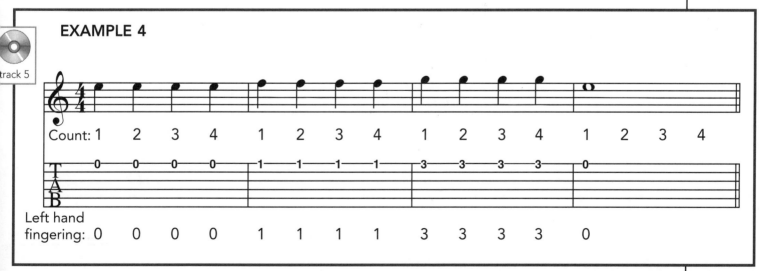

track 5

Count: 1   2   3   4   1   2   3   4   1   2   3   4   1   2   3   4

Left hand
fingering: 0   0   0   0   1   1   1   1   3   3   3   3   0

READING ON THE 2ND STRING

Here are three notes on the 2nd string:

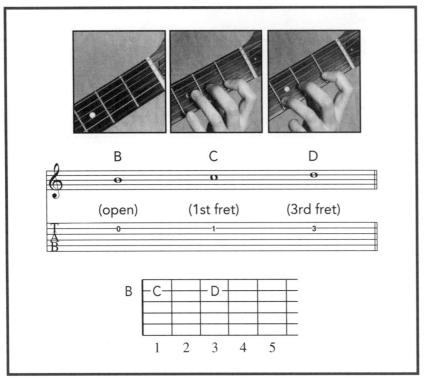

Example 5 consists of half notes (two beats) and whole notes (four beats). Be sure to press down on the string just to the left of the fret and make a good tone without buzzes and rattles.

EXAMPLE 5

track 6

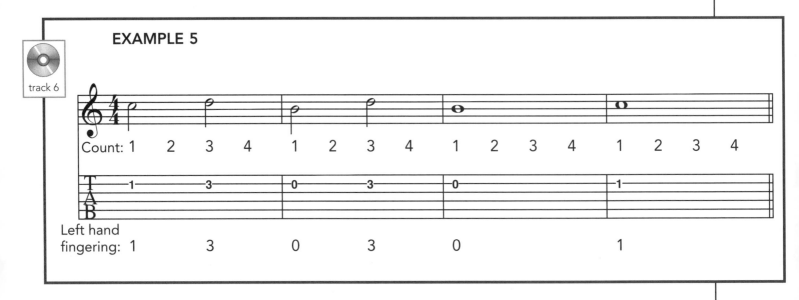

GUITAR MADE EASY!

Example 6 uses quarter notes. Quarter notes get one beat each.

EXAMPLE 6

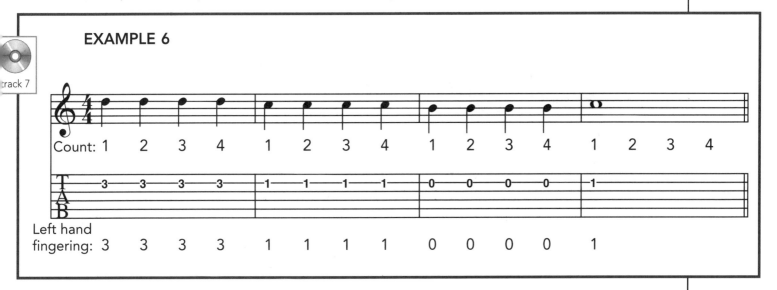

Example 7 uses all the note values you have learned so far: quarter notes (one beat), half notes (two beats) and whole notes (four beats).

EXAMPLE 7

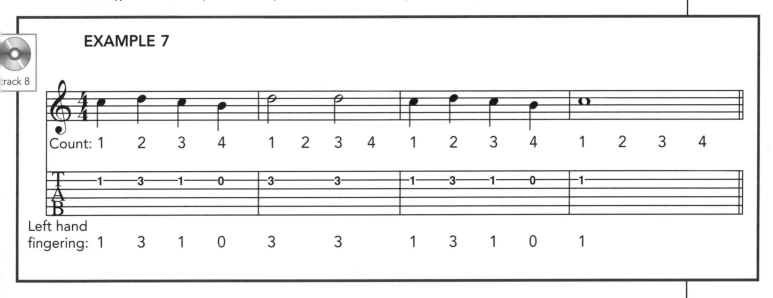

Here's a quarter-note example.

EXAMPLE 8

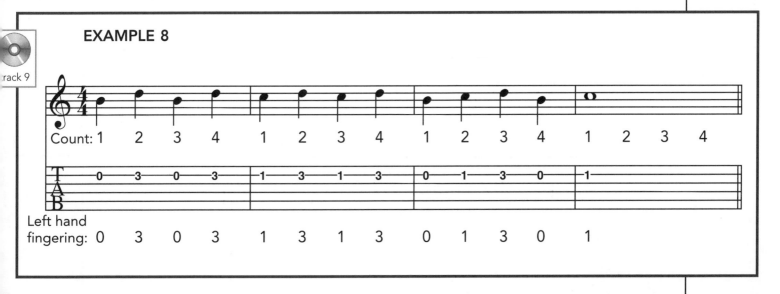

CHAPTER THREE   19

READING ON THE 3RD STRING

Let's move on to the third string now.

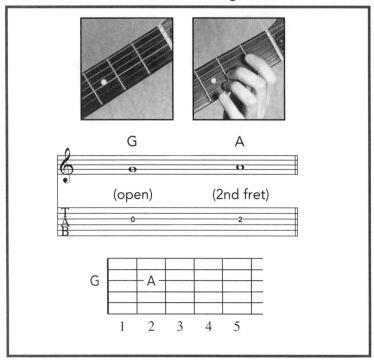

Example 9 uses the 3rd string open (G) and the 3rd string, 2nd fret (A). All the notes are whole notes (four beats.)

EXAMPLE 9

track 10

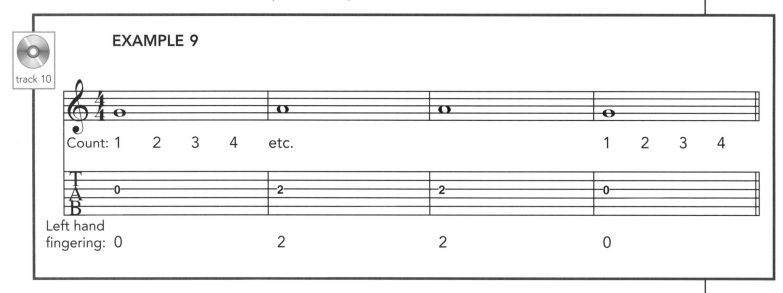

Make sure to hold each half note for its entire duration (two beats).

EXAMPLE 10

Track 11

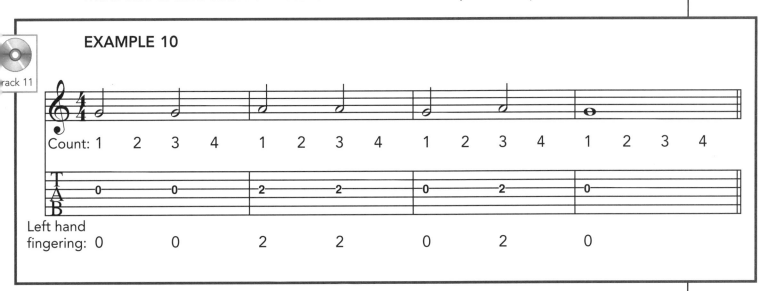

Example 11 contains quarter notes (one beat each) and one whole note (4 beats). Example 12 mixes quarter notes with half notes. Remember that it is always helpful to count aloud when playing these examples. It will help you develop a good sense of rhythm.

EXAMPLE 11

Track 12

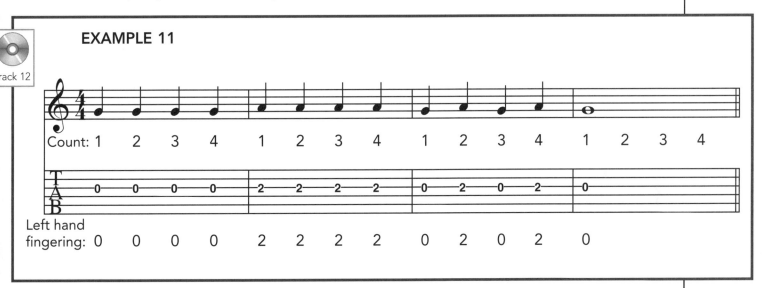

Example 12 contains notes on the 2nd and 3rd strings.

EXAMPLE 12

Track 13

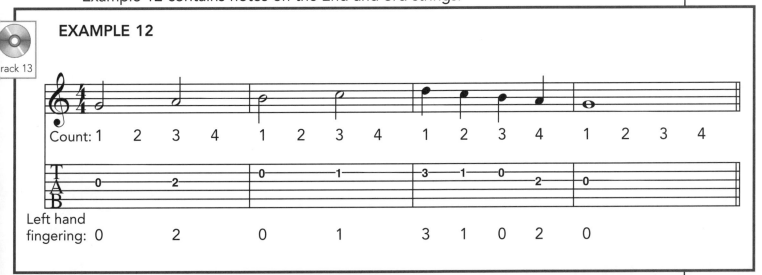

CHAPTER THREE 21

Here is a tune containing notes played on the 1st, 2nd and 3rd strings. Work through it slowly. Saying the names of the notes aloud as you play will help you to learn the piece.

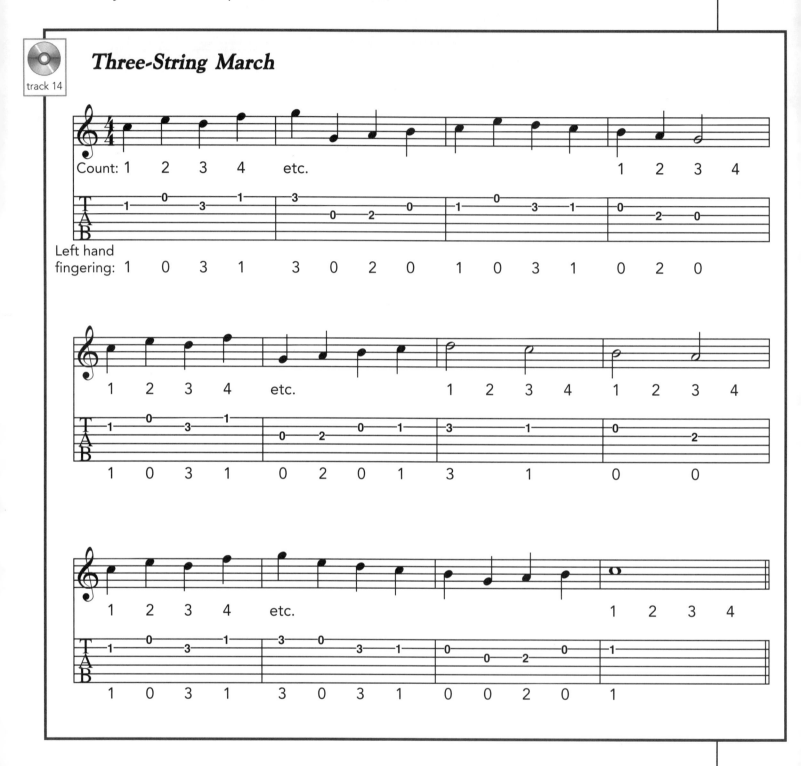

Three-String March

THREE-STRING CHORDS

So far, we have dealt with single-note playing. Now the real fun starts! We are going to talk about *chords*—playing three or more notes at the same time. This is an important step towards learning how to play your favorite songs.

Let's start with some chords that are played on only three strings. We'll work our way up to chords on all six strings soon enough.

CHORD DIAGRAMS

A *chord diagram* is a picture of the fretboard. The vertical lines represent the strings and the horizontal lines represent the frets. The dots are placed on the fret(s) where your finger(s) should be placed. The number directly above the corresponding string tells you which finger to use. In the example below, place your 1st finger on the 1st fret of the 2nd string. The x's above the 4th, 5th and 6th strings tell us *not* to play those strings.

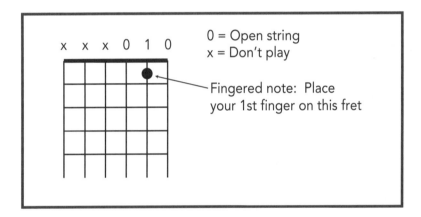

Below is an easy version of a C Major chord. Place your 1st finger on the 1st fret of the 2nd string and strum from the 3rd string down towards the floor. Try to make the first three strings sound simultaneously. Make sure each note is ringing clearly. If you have trouble making the 1st string ring, stand your 1st finger up on its tip.

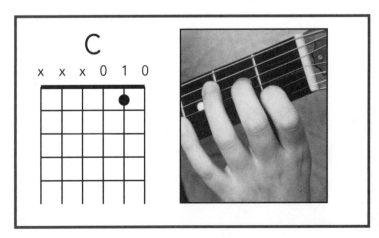

This is an E Minor chord. This is every beginner's favorite chord to play! To play this chord, just strum the open strings, from the third string down.

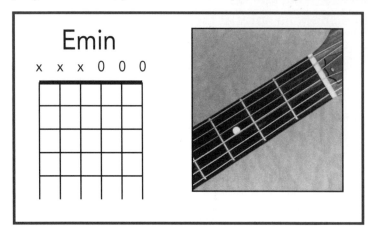

Here is a G Major chord. To play this chord, put your 3rd finger on the 3rd fret of the 1st string. Strum from the 3rd string down.

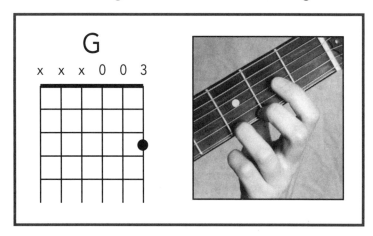

This is a D7 chord. To play this chord, you place your 2nd finger on the 2nd fret of the 3rd string. Then, place your 1st finger on the 1st fret of the 2nd string. Finally, place your 3rd finger on the 2nd fret of the 1st string. Strum from the 3rd string down. Or, you can make it sound fuller by including the open 4th string.

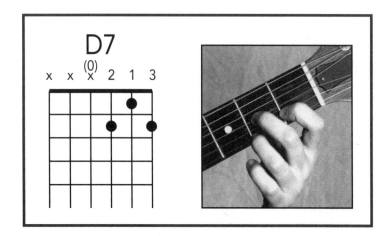

STRUMMING

Now that we've gone over some chords, what's next? Strumming. You will often see chord progressions written with rhythms to be played underneath the chords.

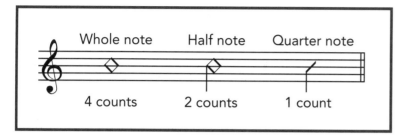

Let's start with some basic strumming patterns. For this example, we are going to play all the chords as whole notes. Each chord will be held out for four beats.

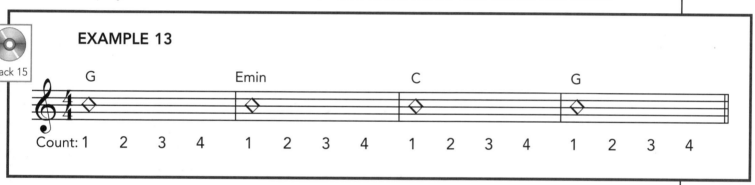

Example two contains half notes and whole notes. Play these examples slowly. Try to change the chords without stopping.

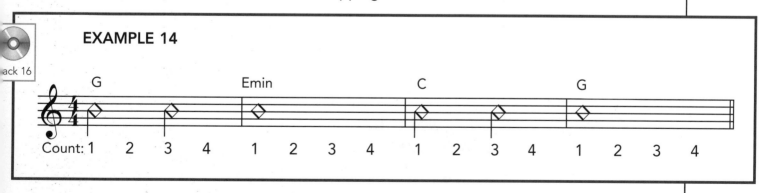

Example 15 introduces a quarter-note strumming pattern. Count aloud to help keep your place in the music. Having good rhythm is essential to being a good guitarist.

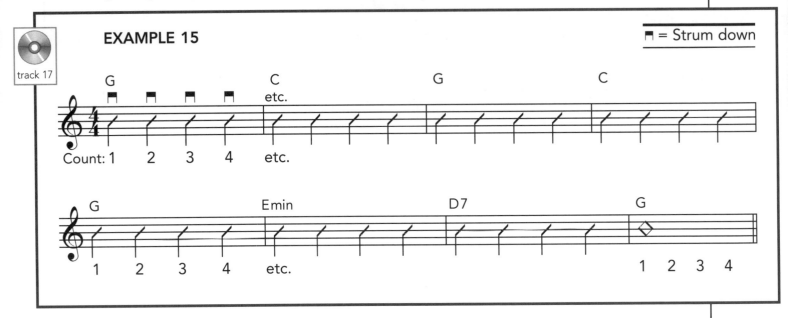

EXAMPLE 15

track 17

■ = Strum down

Example 16 includes the D7 chord.

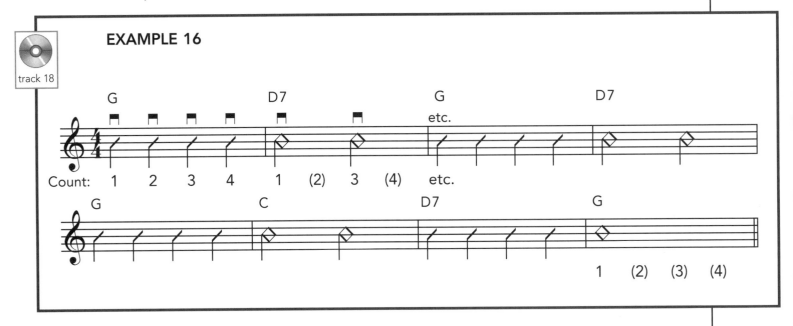

EXAMPLE 16

track 18

Remember to play slowly and be patient with yourself. You can't learn to play overnight. Learning to play guitar is a physical activity. That's why it is important to *practice consistently*. You are training your muscles! If your were running in a marathon, you would train for it. You wouldn't expect your body to be able to perform without running in the weeks leading up to the marathon! So don't expect to be flying over the frets in one week—but it will happen if you practice consistently. It will take some time to get your fingers to do what you want them to do with ease.

READING ON THE 4TH STRING

Here are three notes on the 4th string:

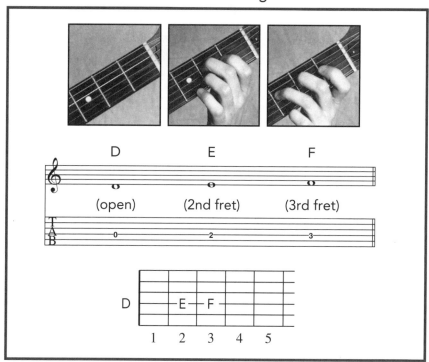

Example 17 has all the note values we have worked on so far: whole notes, half notes and quarter notes.

EXAMPLE 17

track 19

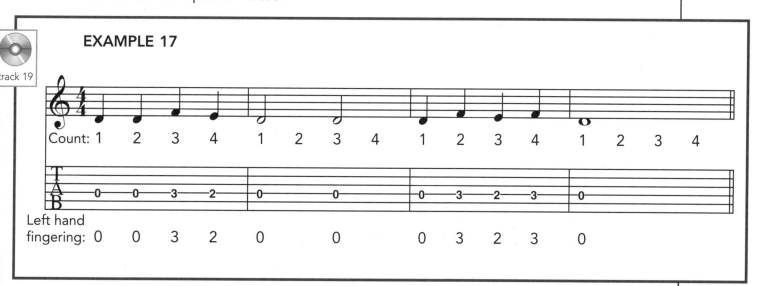

NEW RHYTHM—EIGHTH NOTES

An eighth note lasts for half of a beat. You can fit two eighth notes into any beat. Individual eighth notes have a stem and a flag. When there are consecutive eighth notes, they are *beamed* together.

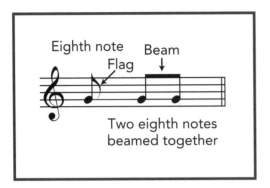

Here is an easy way to understand eighth notes. We often tap our feet when we play or listen to music. Each tap has two parts: the *downbeat* (when the foot is on the floor), and the *upbeat* (when the foot is up in the air). To play eighth notes, play on the downbeats and the upbeats.

Example 18contains eighth notes. Count each measure like so: "1–&–2–&–3–&–4–&."

Example 19 will give you more practice with eighth notes.

LEDGER LINES

The notes on the 5th and 6th strings are written below the staff. To write these notes, we use *ledger lines*. Ledger lines are lines drawn above or below the staff to extend the staff higher or lower.

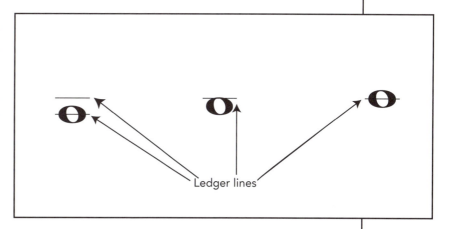

Ledger lines

READING ON THE 5TH STRING.

Here are three notes on the 5th string:

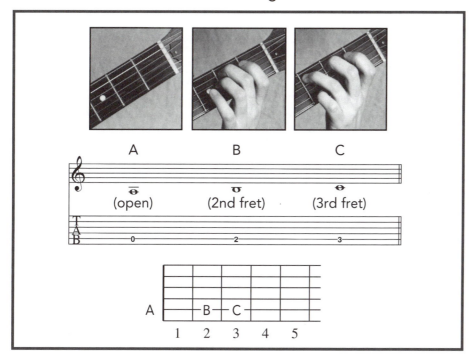

A	B	C
(open)	(2nd fret)	(3rd fret)

Example 20 is a study of the notes on the 5th string using whole notes.

EXAMPLE 20

Track 22

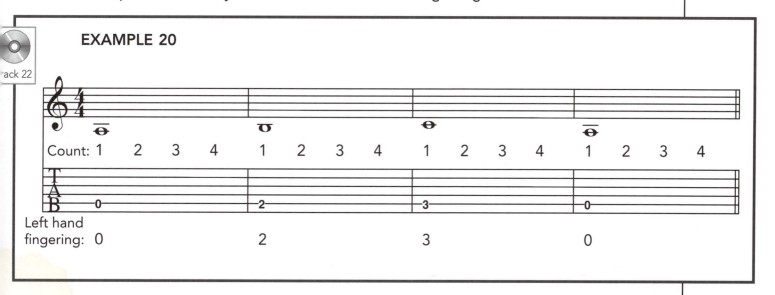

Count: 1 2 3 4   1 2 3 4   1 2 3 4   1 2 3 4

Left hand
fingering: 0   2   3   0

Example 21 mixes half notes and quarter notes and ends with a whole note. As you make progress in this book, make sure to go back and review material from earlier in the book.

EXAMPLE 21

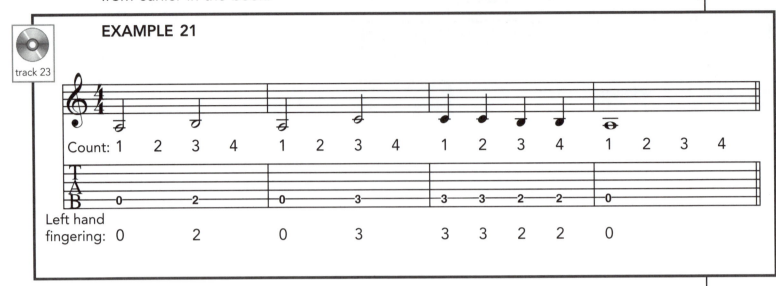

Example 22 mixes all of the note values you have learned. Example 23 contains notes on the 4th and 5th strings. Count carefully!

EXAMPLE 22

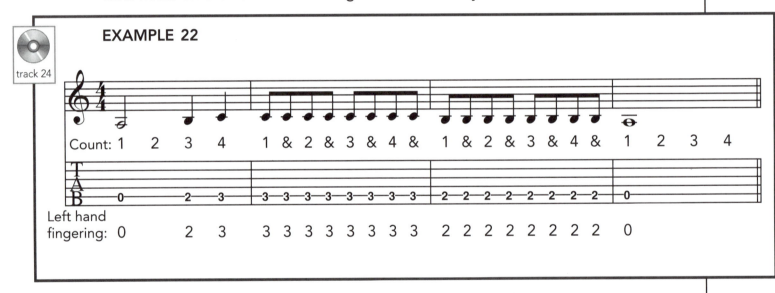

EXAMPLE 23

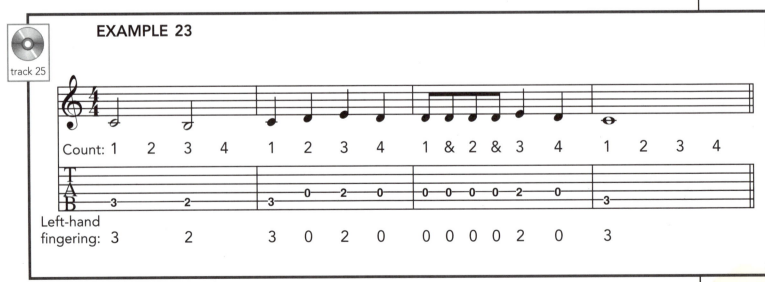

GUITAR *MADE EASY!*

READING ON THE 6TH STRING

Here are three notes on the 6th string. As with the 5th string, the notes on the 6th string are written below the staff with ledger lines.

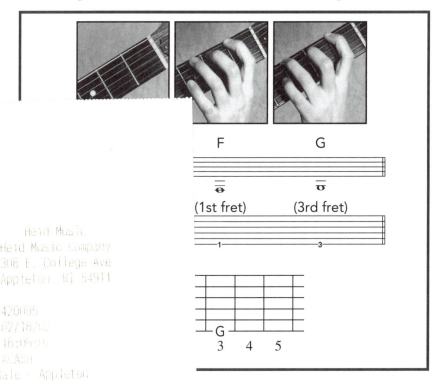

...te study of the notes on the 6th string. Remember ...heir full duration of four beats each.

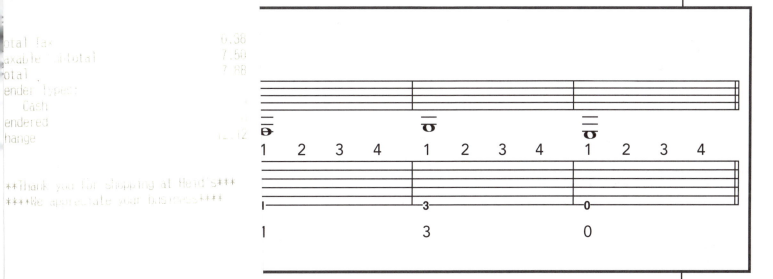

Example 25 will give you more practice reading the notes on the 6th string.

EXAMPLE 25

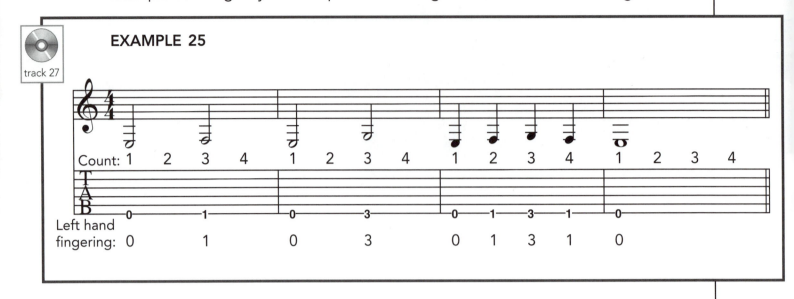

Feel free to write the names of the notes above the examples. This can be helpful when learning to read ledger lines.

EXAMPLE 26

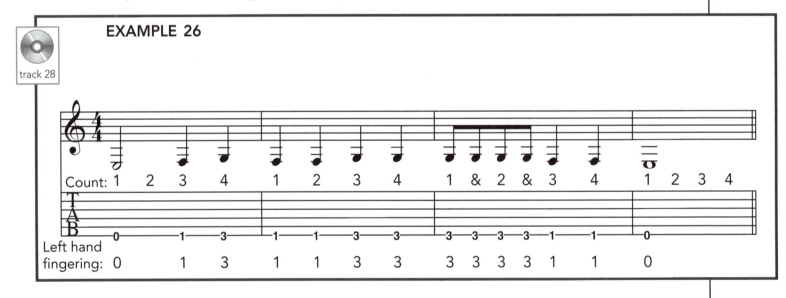

Example 27 contains notes on the 5th and 6th strings.

EXAMPLE 27

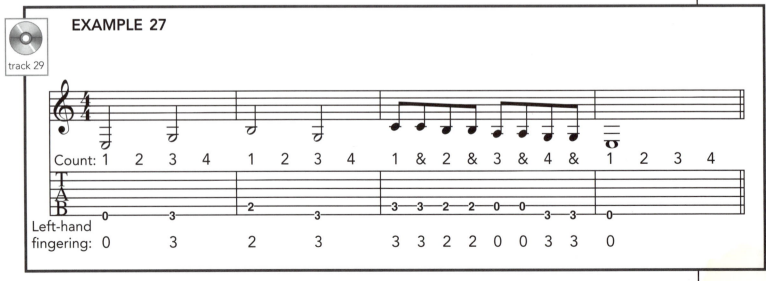

Here is an example using notes from the 4th, 5th and 6th strings. Work through this one slowly. With practice, reading ledger lines will become easier.

Way Down Low

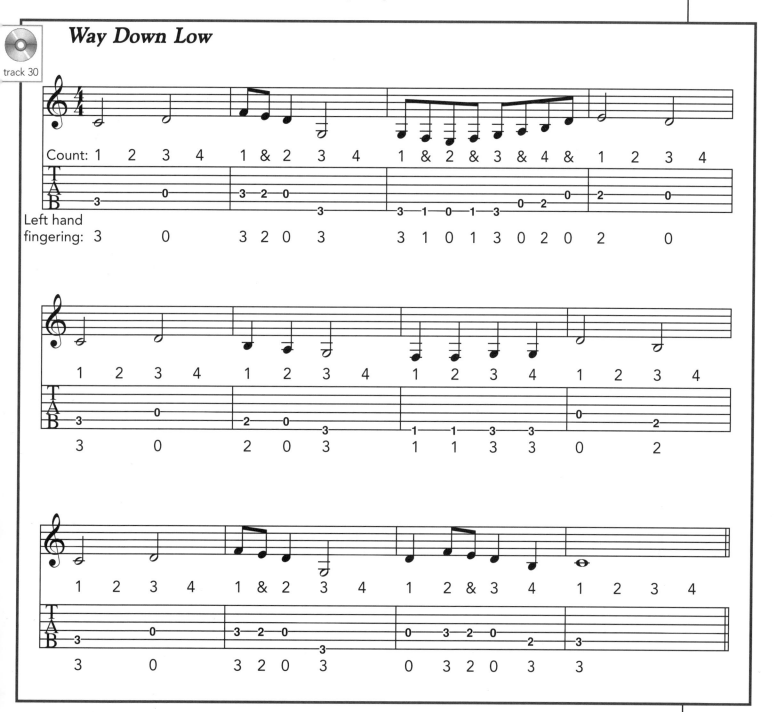

Let's try to play some chords on all six strings.

Here is a full E Minor chord. Put your 2nd finger on the 2nd fret of the 5th string. Place your 3rd finger on the 2nd fret of the 4th string. Strum all six strings. You can use your 1st and 2nd fingers instead if you like.

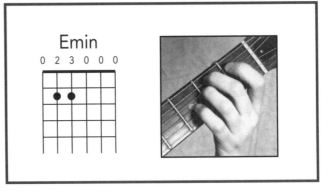

The G Major chord has two possibilities for fingering. You should practice it both ways because the first fingering is better for some songs, while the second fingering works in other contexts.

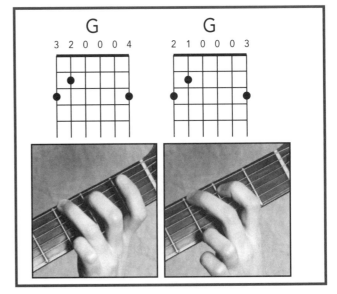

For this full C Major chord fingering, it is very important to keep your fingers curled so that they don't bump into adjacent strings and keep them from ringing clearly.

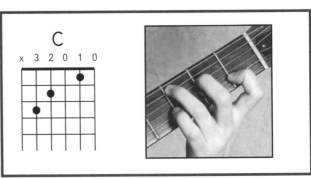

Here is a D Major chord. Remember to curl the left-hand fingers. Be careful not play the open 6th string (E) with this chord. The E note will clash with the chord. Instead, strum from the 5th string down.

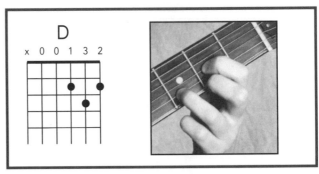

Let's learn some strumming patterns with these chords.

Example 28 is a strumming pattern with eighth notes on the second and fourth beats of the measure. It is best to play these eighth note strums with a down stroke (⊓) on the down beat and an up stroke (∨) on the up beat. Follow the picking pattern above the example.

EXAMPLE 28

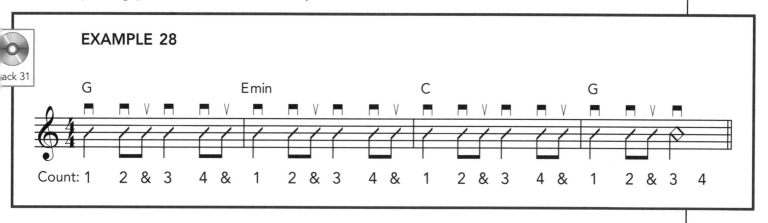

Example 29 consists of a quarter note on the first beat of every measure, followed by eighth notes on the second, third and fourth beats. Example 30 has eighth notes on the fourth beat of the first three measures.

EXAMPLE 29

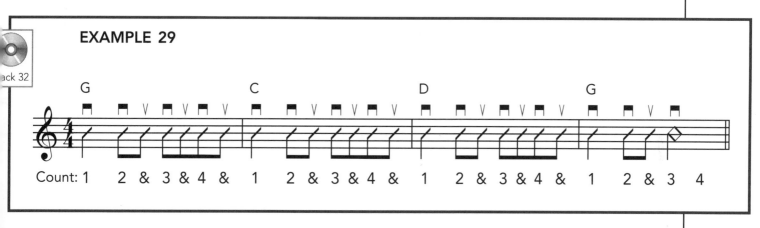

EXAMPLE 30

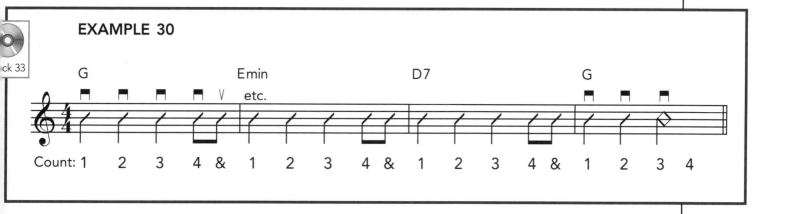

¾ TIME

So far, we have been working in 4/4 time. The next examples are in 3/4 time, also known as *waltz time*. In 3/4 time, there are three beats in every measure. Count it like this: one–two–three, one–two–three, one–two–three, etc.

As with 4/4 time, the top number indicates the number of beats per measure and the bottom number indicates which note value gets one beat.

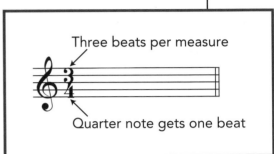

Three beats per measure

Quarter note gets one beat

Examples 31–33 are strumming patterns in 3/4 time.
Count aloud as you practice these examples.

EXAMPLE 31

track 34

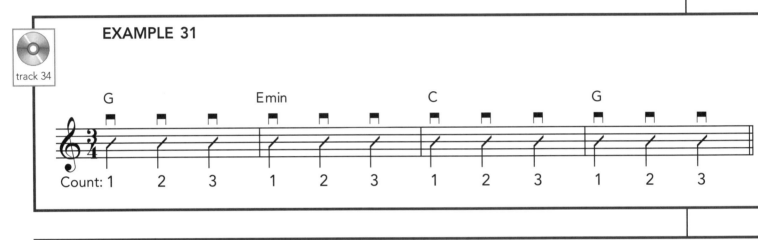

EXAMPLE 32

track 35

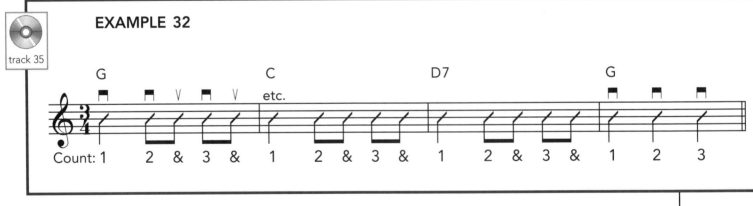

EXAMPLE 33

track 36

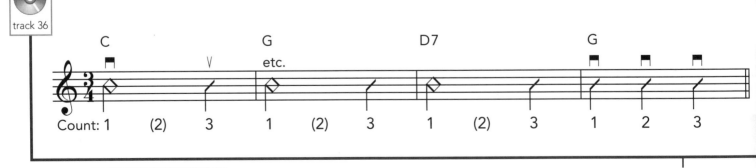

The final part of the book consists of some songs for you to play. Each song has two corresponding strumming patterns on the following page. If you have a friend or family member who also plays guitar, try playing duets. One person can play the melody. The other person can play the chords. In order to play these songs, there are a few new concepts to learn.

RESTS

Rests indicate various lengths of silence in music.

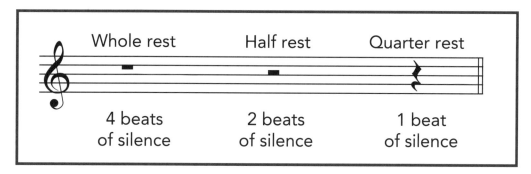

TIES

When two notes of the same pitch are tied together with a curved line, a note that is equal to the total value of both pitches is created. Pick the note once and hold for the duration of both the tied notes.

DOTTED NOTES

When a dot is placed directly after a note, it lengthens the note's value by one half of its original value. For instance, a dotted half note would be held for three counts.

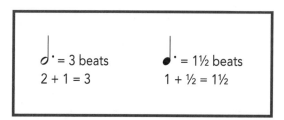

Learn the melody to this beautiful folk song. On the following page, there are two accompaniment strumming patterns that go with it. If you have the CD that is available for this book you can play along.

Amazing Grace

EASY STRUMMING PATTERN-AMAZING GRACE

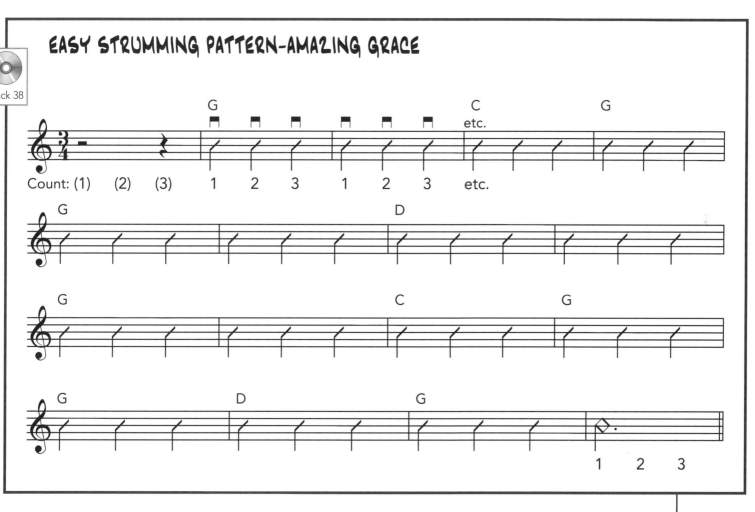

Count: (1)   (2)   (3)   1   2   3   1   2   3   etc.

EIGHTH-NOTE STRUMMING PATTERN-AMAZING GRACE

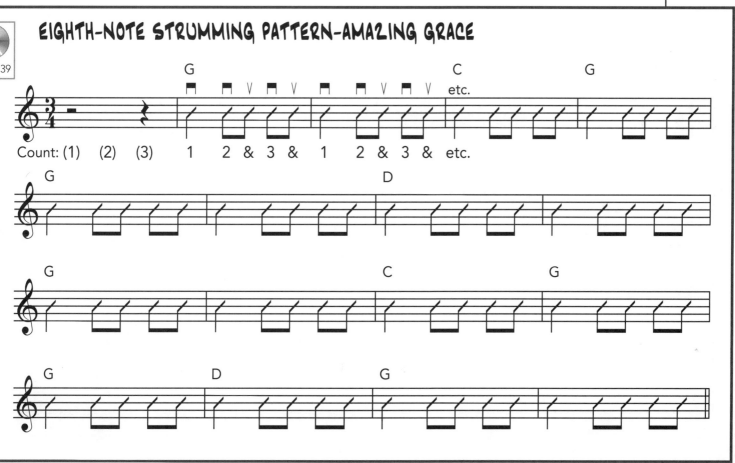

Count: (1)   (2)   (3)   1   2 & 3 &   1   2 & 3 &   etc.

track 40

WILL THE CIRCLE BE UNBROKEN

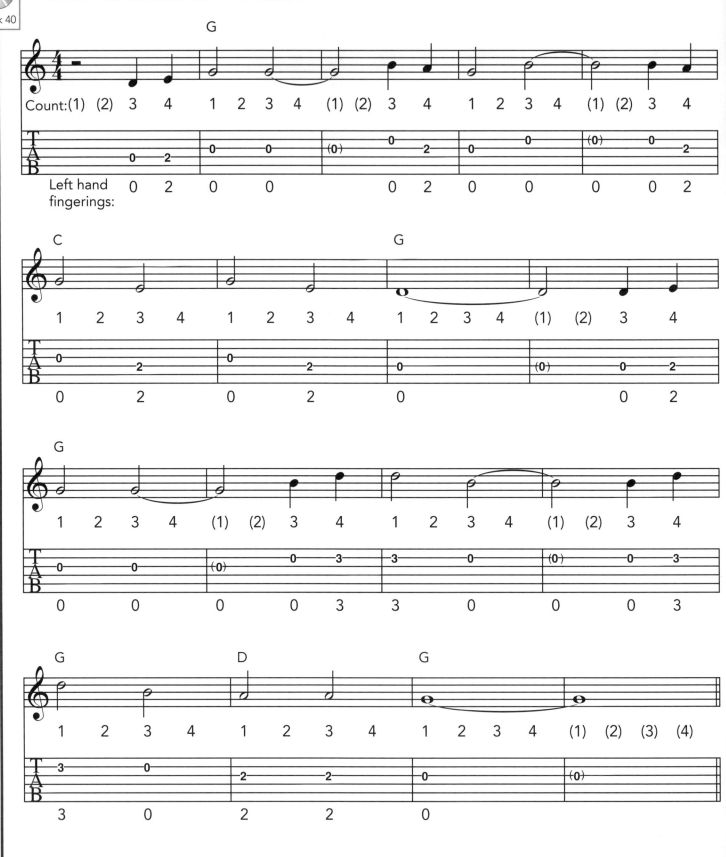

EASY STRUMMING PATTERN-WILL THE CIRCLE BE UNBROKEN

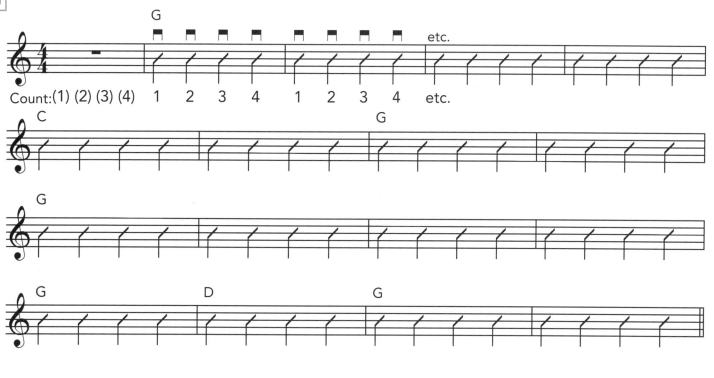

Count: (1) (2) (3) (4)   1   2   3   4   1   2   3   4   etc.

track 42

EIGHTH-NOTE STRUMMING PATTERN-WILL THE CIRCLE BE UNBROKEN

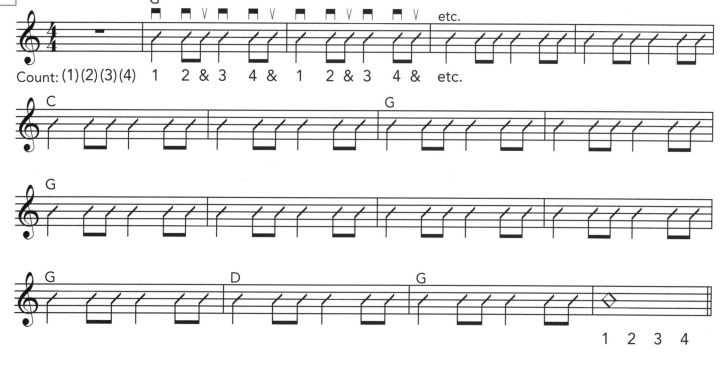

Count: (1) (2) (3) (4)   1   2 & 3   4 &   1   2 & 3   4 &   etc.

track 43

BANKS OF THE OHIO

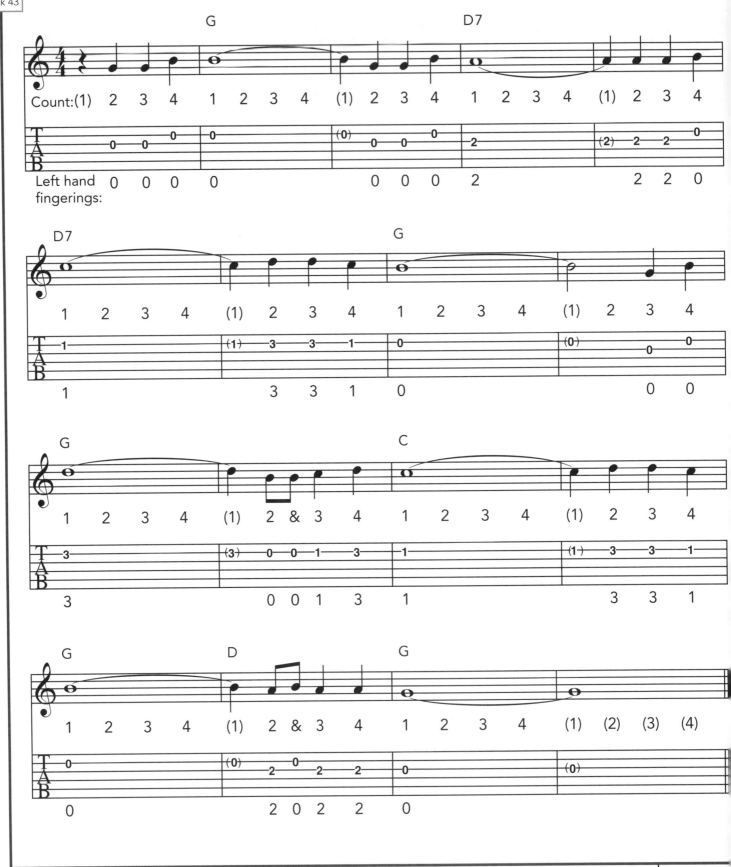

GUITAR MADE EASY!

EASY STRUMMING PATTERN-BANKS OF THE OHIO

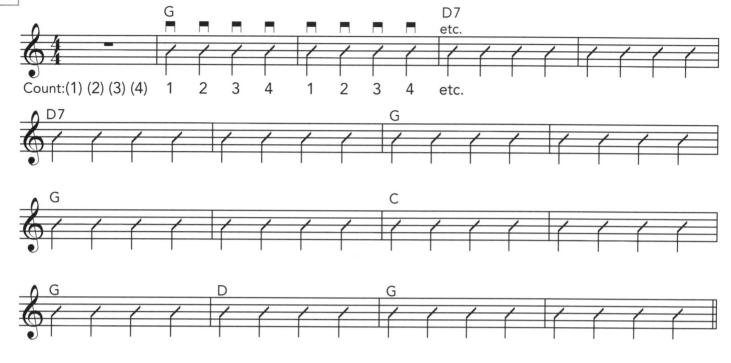

EIGHTH-NOTE STRUMMING PATTERN-BANKS OF THE OHIO

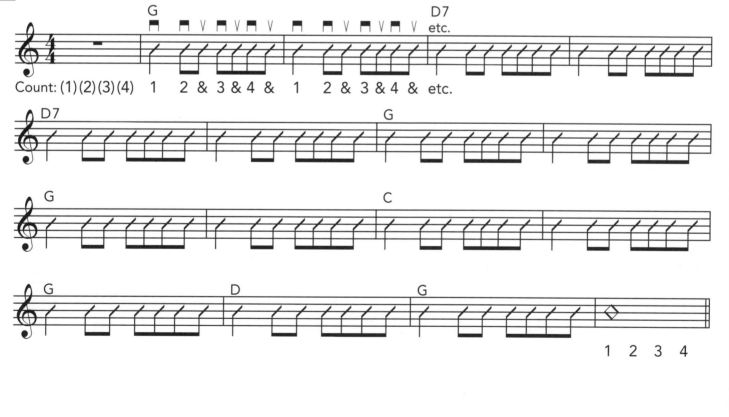

WHEN THE SAINTS GO MARCHING IN

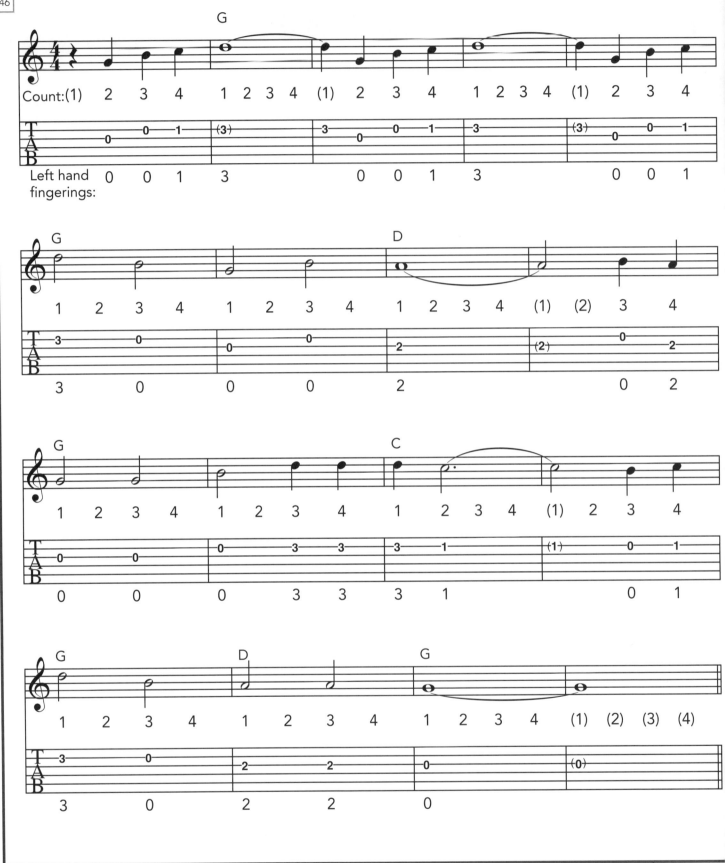

EASY STRUMMING PATTERN-WHEN THE SAINTS GO MARCHING IN

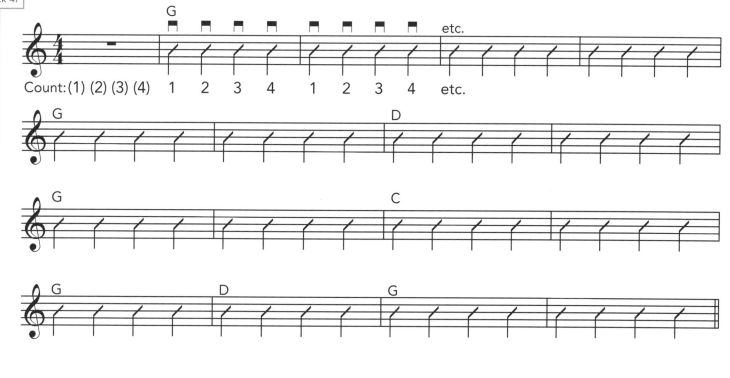

Count: (1) (2) (3) (4)   1   2   3   4   1   2   3   4   etc.

EIGHTH-NOTE STRUMMING PATTERN-WHEN THE SAINTS GO MARCHING IN

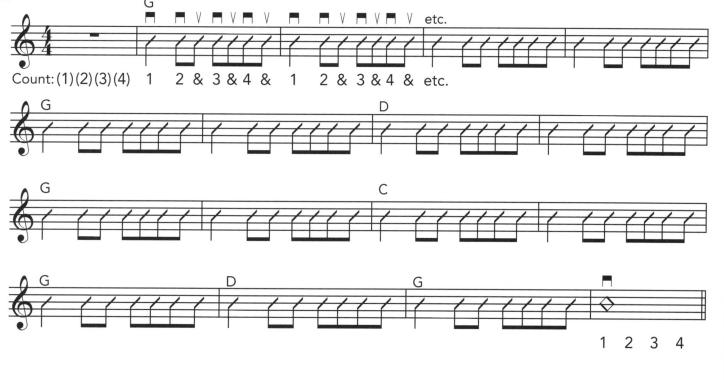

Count: (1) (2) (3) (4)   1   2 & 3 & 4 &   1   2 & 3 & 4 &   etc.

CHAPTER FIVE   45

Congratulations! You have completed *Guitar Made Easy!* You've made an important step towards becoming a great guitarist. Remember this is only the beginning. It is important to build upon the progress you have made. Find a good private teacher. Listen to your favorite guitar players and absorb their music. Find other books, such as *Beginning Rock Guitar* (published by the National Guitar Workshop and Alfred Publishing) to learn from. Good luck and keep practicing!

Dave Matthews *Band emerged in the 1990's with a jazz-inflected rock sound driven by funky acoustic guitar riffs. Matthews released a live album of duo performances with Tim Reynolds, "Live at Luther College, 1996." Reynolds' eclectic and fluid lead work combined with Matthews' driving rhythms and songwriting, create a benchmark of modern acoustic rock.*

APPENDIX Left-Hand Technqiue

The job of the left hand is to press the strings at the appropriate frets in order to produce the desired tones.

THE LEFT-HAND FINGERS

The fingers are indicated as follows:

Index .... 1 ...... 1st finger
Middle ..... 2 ...... 2nd finger
Ring .... 3 ...... 3rd finger
Pinky .... 4 ...... 4th finger

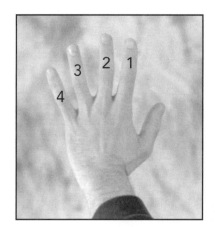

THE POSITION

Your thumb should be around the back of the neck of the guitar, pointing upward behind your middle finger.

When playing a single note or chord, your fingers should be arched so the notes are being played by your fingertips. This prevents your fingers from accidentally interfering with or touching another string.

Place your fingers just to the left of the frets. Do not play with your fingers directly on the fret wire. Placing fingers too far to the left of the fret may cause buzzes or muted notes.

Your wrist should be bent towards the floor. Your palm should not touch the neck of the guitar.

Trim your left-hand fingernails. You can't play guitar if the nails on your left hand are too long.